STYLISH LIVING
in South Africa

STYLISH LIVING
in South Africa

photography by Craig Fraser
text by Suzanne Brenner

First published in 1999 by
Struik Publishers (Pty) Ltd
(A member of Struik New Holland Publishing (Pty) Ltd)
Cornelis Struik House
80 McKenzie Street
Cape Town 8001

Reg. No. 54/00965/07

ISBN 1 86872 473 5

10 9 8 7 6 5 4 3 2

Project Manager: Linda de Villiers
Editor: Laura Milton
Designer: Petal Palmer
Design Assistant: Matthew Ibbotson
Photographer: Craig Fraser
Photographer's Assistant: Oliver Hugo

Reproduction by Hirt & Carter Cape (Pty) Ltd
Printed and bound by Tien Wah Press (Pte) Limited, Singapore

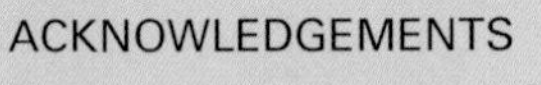

ACKNOWLEDGEMENTS
Copyright in a number of photographs rests with the magazines in which the photographs were first published, or by whom the photographer was commissioned. The publishers wish to thank the following magazines for permission to reproduce photographs:
Elle Decoration (South Africa) for photographs on pages 12, 21 (left, top and bottom, and bottom right), 35 and 40
Elle Decoration (UK) for the photograph on page 31
FairLady for photographs on pages 8/9, 10 (main picture and inset), 14 (top right and bottom left), 19, 23, 32, 52 (top left), 54 and 118 (top right)
Habitat for photographs on the front cover, pages 2/3, 11 (main picture and inset), 14 (bottom right), 15, 18, 22, 34, 38, 39, 41, 46, 48, 49, 50, 51, 52 (top right and bottom right), 53 (inset), 55, 56, 57 (top left, top right, bottom left and bottom right), 58, 59, 62/63, 64, 65 (left), 65 (top right and bottom right), 68 (top left, top right and bottom right), 69, 74 (left and right), 77, 78, 83, 116, 118 (top left), 119, 120, 121 (left and right), 122/123, 124, 125, 127, 130 (top left, bottom right and bottom left), 132, 133, 140 (top left) and 141
House and Leisure for the photograph on page 13

contents

Dedicated to my parents, Colin and Julia Fraser,
for their inspiration and support.

foreword

In the late 1980s Faith Popcorn, the well-known New York-based trend guru, formulated her theory of 'cocooning', predicting that people in the Western world would become more interested in 'house, home, art, culture and environmental issues; and that they would spend more time in their own very personal nests'. Well, she was absolutely right, because by the mid-1990s the interest in houses and decorating had burgeoned. And, as we enter the new millennium, it is clear that interior decorating and design have never been appreciated and understood by so many people on a global scale.

The history of the discipline and the industry that it has spawned in South Africa is indeed a fascinating matter for study. This book – creatively photographed by Craig Fraser — will help to illustrate just how far our local industry has progressed, to the level that we are surely on a par with most major countries in the world.

To South Africans of all groups 'house and home' have never been more important – we all want to live in secure, comfortable and yet appealing personal environments. Within the covers of this book you will find plenty of inspiring ideas. Wherever you may dream to live in this 'world in one country' of ours, there is a signature here to suit most handwritings.

COLIN AINSWORTH SHARP
Publisher/Managing Editor
Habitat magazine
Johannesburg

living in the city

TRYING TO DETERMINE WHAT CONSTITUTES TYPICAL South African style and taste is no easy task. Within each of the country's cities, whether in Cape Town, Durban or Johannesburg, locals demonstrate their own unique interpretation of urban homes. As will be seen in the pages of this book, almost anything goes – from minimalist simplicity to African ethnic and variations on Eastern and Western themes. New influences in South Africa have opened doors to a wide cross-pollination of ideas and cultures, energizing previously compartmentalized lifestyles. City living can encompass whatever you want it to: wide open spaces, compact clusters, high-rises, low-rises, lock-up-and-go apartments, lofts, bachelor pads and spacious mansions. Eclectic mixes of colour, texture, materials, architecture and interior design – this is city living in South Africa.

PAGE 8: For this home-owner, living in Cape Town means a view of Lion's Head from the kitchen, where chrome and stainless steel introduce industrial modernity.

ABOVE: The fireplace offers winter warmth while a pair of armchairs in heavy, off-white fabric provide comfort. A thick, black throw is on hand for additional insulation. The roughly woven rug contributes to the homely atmosphere.

RIGHT: A riempie bench rests between two large windows which let in an abundance of natural light. Basketwork under the side tables and on the wall adds cottage style, while a lone blue vase injects some colour.

RIGHT: An exotic mask adorns an unusual, curved, modern wooden drawer unit. Silk cushion covers of interwoven beige and black mix happily with the subtle floral motifs of the couch fabric. Cretestone walls are sealed with clear lacquer.

ABOVE: There's an eclectic mix of shapes, colours, textures and designs in this living area which opens onto a balcony overlooking Balie Bay in Cape Town. A beautiful wood-framed door with a curved handle and an etched, sand-blasted glass panel in the centre opens into the interleading dining and sitting rooms. A pair of chunky armchairs face couches upholstered in yellow, textured leather. The blonde wood of the modern, custom-made coffee and side tables echoes that of the door frame.

Natural light abounds in this carefully orchestrated, almost all-white setting, which gains added volume from a free-standing mirror in a dark frame. A narrow, horizontal window runs almost the entire length of the room. Ensuring privacy, it is positioned just below ceiling height. The couch below it is mounted on wheels for easy mobility. The standing lamp in the corner replicates the shape of the lampshade hanging from the ceiling. Chrome, steel and a dash of wood are used intermittently to break the stark whiteness and add visual interest in terms of matte and shiny surfaces.

Loft living à la New York is a fast-growing trend along Cape Town's Atlantic Seaboard area, where lofts are proving to be the ideal lock-up-and-go pads for out-of-towners. In this example, a heavy steel door opens into a triple-volume space of white and beige minimalism. With low maintenance a priority, a bare cement floor is practical, attractive and cool – but not inhospitable. And the large sofa looks tempting with its throws at either end to cater for changeable Cape weather.

CLOCKWISE, FROM TOP LEFT: Nothing distracts from the function of this dining room where firelight, bucket-seated dining chairs, rough-textured, industrial-style pillars and bare wooden floors set the scene.

Light and space predominate and the expansive glass-bricked wall is the focus. While sparsely furnished, the wood brings warmth to the area.

This dining area leads off the lounge shown on page 11 (inset). The deep violet shade of the chairs mirrors the rich colours of the sea and the glorious sunset. A modern light fitting spotlights a bowl of lemons, which echoes the yellow colour of the leather couches in the lounge.

The combination of white and warm wood continues in the dining area – an extension of the lounge shown on page 10. A *faux* walnut finish distinguishes the corner cupboard, and slipcovers disguise folding chairs made of steel.

Another view of the dining area shown on the opposite page (top left) illustrates the relationship between the dining room and the kitchen (featured on page 30).

This is the dining area of a light and airy loft apartment, exhibiting the same simple, clean lines which are to be seen in the bedroom shown on page 25 (bottom right) and the lounge on page 36 (inset). The same combination of colours and finishes is used throughout the home, and rugged and smooth textures are juxtaposed to create the desired effect. While Eastern-style sliding screens are used to separate the various living areas or to grant privacy when necessary, the fact that the blonde wood frames contain 'panes' of almost transparent, textured white paper, means that all-important light is allowed through. The rustic wall finish is echoed in the rough treatment used on the wooden table, and the stylish wall unit sets the tone for the elegant chairs and smooth, polished floor.

A spectacular view of the ocean is a vital element of this lounge which overlooks Clifton's Fourth Beach in Cape Town. Shadows form part of the decor as bright sunlight filters through slatted, maple doors which can be folded away completely to allow an uninterrupted view of the sea. An inviting lounger upholstered in warm but pale yellow is perfectly placed for sociability or – on rotation – for quietly communing with nature.

Elegance and simplicity rule in this bathroom. A pale green sand-blasted glass basin perches atop a wooden counter which matches the shade of the wooden Venetian blinds. A mirror that reaches the ceiling creates the illusion of a much larger space, and unusual chrome fittings add a touch of class.

Dark furniture contrasts with the pale cretestone walls and wooden floors in this lounge which combines modernity and tradition.The setting is enhanced by steel columns and by the light that streams in through the steel-framed windows. Full-length blinds become a feature while 'portholes' just beneath the ceiling are quaintly decorative rather than functional. Rounded shapes are used subtly to contrast with the multitude of sharp angles and straight lines.

LEFT, TOP AND BOTTOM, AND BOTTOM RIGHT: White is the predominant colour in this house, also featured on page 12. Box chairs, steel, chrome and black leather contrast starkly with the ceilings, walls and floor in this studio. Carefully selected black-and-white photographs – framed alternately in black or white – are propped up on a ledge. At certain times of the day, the skylight creates austere, linear shadows.

TOP, RIGHT: In this view of the loft living area featured on page 13, clear Cape light pours through the window. Wonderfully straightforward side tables on casters can easily be moved together to form a larger coffee table. Round, woven baskets complete the symmetry.

Bringing a bit of the outdoors indoors, an atrium forms an extension to this lounge, also featured on page 11 (inset) and page 14. On sultry days and nights, the sliding glass doors can be opened for ventilation. Cement slabs and white pebbles offset delicate greenery, contrasting with the earthy brown and rich golden yellow tones of the adjacent furniture – colours which are repeated in the large paintings.

A hint of Japanese minimalism comes into play in this tranquil bedroom. Natural tones and textures provide a peaceful setting – from the linen-covered easy chairs through to the coir carpet, terracotta pots and a low, beechwood bed. A paper screen adds to the Eastern feel.

Although the furnishings are sparse and functional, a feeling of warmth pervades this A-frame bedroom where the white-painted roof-beams are juxtaposed with natural wood and undisguised brick. A square window recessed into the wall above the bed provides much-needed light, as well as a clever showcase for an ornamental bird. Aptly, the main focus of the room is the ample-sized bed.

FAR LEFT: Floor-to-ceiling doors open onto utter simplicity. Bare walls and a coir carpet blend with the subtle use of colour in the wide, beige and white stripes of the bed linen. At night, adjustable overhead fittings allow light to be directed where it is needed.

LEFT, TOP: Timber hues offer the only contrast to the stark whiteness. Abundant natural light, controlled by a Venetian blind, plays an important role where furnishing is minimal.

LEFT, BOTTOM: Natural tones combine to create a relaxed ambience in this bedroom with an Eastern influence. A full-length mirror and a mirror above the dressing table are additional sources of reflected light. The eye-catching, suspended ceiling adds warmth, intimacy and distinctive style to the room, while the sliding door ensures optimal use of space.

Delicate, slide-along, low-voltage lights are suspended from cables along the unusual, rough slab ceiling. The smooth, glass table-top reveals a pattern of small squares, characteristic of reinforced safety glass. This design element is echoed in the small, square tiles on the far wall of the kitchen. The sculpture in the window recalls the figure in the painting in terms of colour and shape.

OPPOSITE PAGE: A free-standing fireplace promises warmth and comfort in this living room. Expanded steel mesh 'walls' extend from floor to ceiling on either side, separating areas of the home visually, yet allowing the warm air to circulate freely.

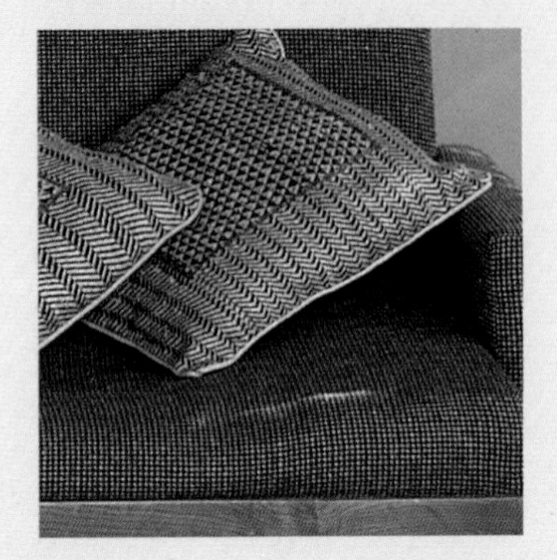

Split levels contribute to the wonderful sense of space and depth in this open-plan lounge which leads off the dining room featured on page 26. The wooden floor ensures a sense of continuity, while a contemporary, light-coloured three-seater couch and a '50s-style brown couch make a good match.

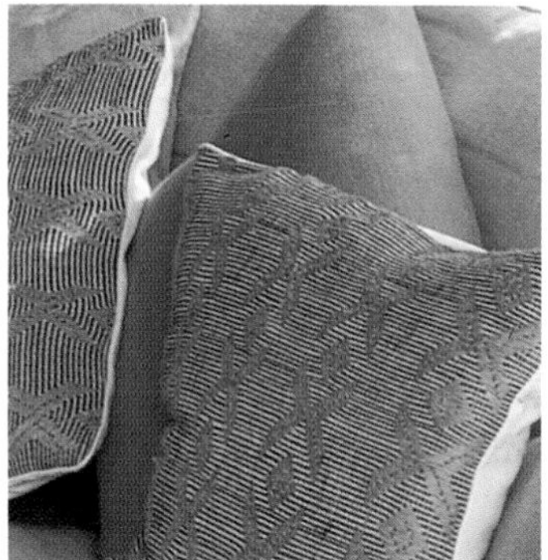

A generous number of soft, comfortable cushions covered in neutral colours – brown, black and beige – interact harmoniously with the lush herb and flower garden and the stone pathway, which the rooms overlook.

A warm wooden counter tops stainless steel cupboards and a floor of industrial metal cladding in this kitchen (featured in completion on page 15) which, at the time of this photograph, was a work in progress. The texture of the lacquered wall is highlighted by natural light which filters through the Venetian blinds and the skylight (inset).

Tones of grey, silver and black make for a no-nonsense industrial-style kitchen. The concrete floor is matched by a lacquered, reinforced concrete worktop. Steel-clad cupboards add to the factory feel and a suspended rod on either side of the extractor fan provides a useful hanging space for essential utensils. Wooden beams support a corrugated iron roof (inset).

A magnificent sea view has been fully exploited by the architect who designed and lives in this ultramodern one-roomed home. He also designed the galvanized metal chairs on the veranda, which are – in the absence of a railing – only there for the brave. A striking metal sculpture is lit at night to great dramatic effect.

Beautiful blonde wood, combined with an unusual colour scheme, creates a warm atmosphere in this semi-formal foyer. The rich, dark green chaise longue acts as a perfect complement to the wall colours, and its sleek shape invites the company of a contemporary standing lamp and table. More traditional, ornate gold frames do not seem at odds with the modernity elsewhere, and contribute to the lavish feel.

A preference for wood – whether painted, stained or natural – is evidenced in this lounge which centres around the fireplace. A high ceiling and loads of light contribute to a feeling of unrestricted space. Visual interest is added by juxtaposing vertical and horizontal lines in the panelled walls and ceiling and slatted blinds – only the bottoms of the chairs providing brief signs of 'cross-hatching'.

ABOVE: On generously sized furniture, pale upholstery and finishes counteract any impression of 'heaviness'.

RIGHT: Bare essentials and muted colours combine to create a serene environment.

OPPOSITE PAGE , LEFT: This fireplace is striking in proportion and simplicity.

OPPOSITE PAGE, RIGHT, TOP: A black-and-white bedroom exhibits a witty, '50s twist.

OPPOSITE PAGE, RIGHT, BOTTOM: A small breakfast table suffices in this high-ceilinged, no-nonsense space.

Kids in wonderland could be the theme of the room featured on this and the following page. The white walls are decorated with favourite characters like Tintin and Snowy, or Asterix and Obelix, while never-forgotten Noddy rests on a green-and-white checked beanbag. The bold designs on the colourful mat are almost incidental in the greater scheme of things. Cheery and child-friendly, the polka-dotted furniture is hand-painted in rainbow hues.

This bedroom for a little prince is dominated by restful blues and greens. A blue-and-white checked blind hangs with surprising ease beside the busy wallpaper featuring planes, cars and trains. Checks are repeated in the lampshades and pillow cases and on the reverse of the duvet cover. The wooden furniture has been hand-painted using dragging, sponging and colour-washing techniques. And for total practicality, the seating unit at the foot of the bed offers great storage space.

Loft living originated in converted factories before architects caught on to the idea of building lofts from scratch. The influence of industrial style is illustrated here, in the uncluttered lines of a simple, but elegantly constructed staircase in metal and wood, drenched in natural light which streams in through expansive windows (inset), left unadorned for maximum effect.

Despite the bare walls, a warm glow pervades this dining room featuring a simple, custom-made glass-topped table with rich-hued, tapered legs. The dining room chairs are formal yet comfortable. The gleaming, stained wooden floor stops at the entrance to the interleading kitchen (not visible), which is given a separate identity by ceramic tiles, which also continue into and up the wall of the guest bathroom.

OPPOSITE PAGE: Stark, sparse simplicity and an industrial feel pervade this modern, city kitchen. Huge slabs of roughly treated cement in tones of grey are offset by black and white. The floor is unadorned cement. In keeping with the near-Spartan approach, the battle-grey balustrade is elegantly uncluttered. Beyond the vast windows – kept bare of curtains or blinds – the views are simply breath-taking.

LEFT, TOP: A different perspective of the kitchen on the opposite page reveals the flow of rooms, plus the scale and proportion of the architecture. The curve of the ceiling is clearly visible here, as it echoes the curve of the kitchen counter.

LEFT, BOTTOM: In the dining room beyond the kitchen (seen at the top of this page, and opposite) blonde wood adds a touch of warmth. And the elegantly curved legs of the chairs, in addition to the striking flowers, offer welcome relief amidst a myriad straight lines.

The wonderful combination of materials is the making of this kitchen. Bare brick walls – that are both practical and attractive – contrast sharply with shiny metal and stainless steel. Tiling is kept to a minimum, and used more for aesthetic rather than practical reasons. In places, the natural colour of the wood is retained to add warmth. The ceiling beams, however, are painted black to create contrast and to pick up the colour of the wall tiles, the door frame, and the bricks forming part of the floor design.

FAR LEFT: The lower storey of the home featured on the previous pages shows the unpainted concrete slab 'ceiling', which lends the interior the feel of an industrial work in progress. A neatly edged wooden floor defines the function of the area around the work station.

LEFT, TOP: The dining area of this natural brick interior showcases an open staircase of metal and wood. High, recessed windows admit light and provide ledges for displaying ornaments. A wine rack occupies the 'dead' space below the stairs.

LEFT, BOTTOM: A structure built of stones separates the fireplace from the surrounding brickwork. The same narrow, vertical window design used in the kitchen of this home (on the opposite page) is repeated here. Again, the successful combination of natural materials – down to the rough, hessian curtains – is the key to creating the look.

living in the country

Country living in South Africa is as varied as the provinces themselves. For some it means an English gentility represented by streams, rivers and trout-fishing; for others it consists of lush tropical conditions, avocados, mangoes, bananas and palm trees or even a home-from-home with an ostrich or two in the barren Karoo. It can be a rambling farm with cattle and domestic animals; a sprawling estate complete with vineyard, or perhaps it is a tiny, thatched cottage on a plot the size of a postage stamp. For many, it is a place to escape the demands of the big city. For others, it's simply home. Country residences are whatever the owners want them to be – they can be found a simple stone's throw from the nearest big city or without proximity to even a small trading store.

PAGE 46: A characterful attic sitting-room-cum-study opens onto a small bedroom. Windows set into the sloping roof admit light in both rooms. A feeling of country comfort is generated by the rough poles, exposed thatch, edge-to-edge matting in natural fibre, and a well-worn but highly polished coffee table.

RIGHT: The epitome of elegance and sophistication, this bedroom is a self-contained haven. A 'floating' wall serves as a 'headboard', allowing free access to the *en suite* bathroom and cupboards on either side of the sleeping area. Creamy yellow walls provide a peaceful backdrop for decor which is sumptuous without being ostentatious. The large bed is gloriously covered with an embroidered and tasselled bedspread and cushions. The neutral shades of the wall-to-wall carpet and furniture give import to the quiet tones of the rug.

Bold use of colour emphasizes the interesting architectural details of the walls and partitioned ceiling of this unusual bedroom. Natural light pours in through the huge panes of the sliding door, enhancing the cheerful, warm tones of the unusual – but successful – mix of patterns in the bedding and rug.

Leading off the bedroom seen on page 48, this spacious bathroom is large enough to accommodate company – as is demonstrated by the presence of the ornate armchair and the cushion on the ledge next to the bath. The Victorian bathtub has been placed on a raised, tiled podium in front of a *trompe l'oeil* mural of a fantasy garden, complete with lemon tree. A vertical row of glass bricks alongside the mural allows in natural light, while the convenient ledge in front also puts towels and reading matter within reach. Glass doors enclose the shower without obstructing the view or breaking up the space visually, and a set of heated towel rails ensures after-bath delight.

Turning a potential 'problem bathroom' into a feast of colour, the owner has opted for a strident shade of clay-red on the walls, which contrast sharply with the baby-blue tiles. Framed photographs with a highly personal significance are carefully arranged above and below a narrow, horizontal window. A selection of pot plants adds delicacy, and meticulous attention to detail is evident in terms of all the bathroom accessories.

CLOCKWISE, FROM TOP LEFT:
This cheerful, multi-purpose room features oodles of natural light, and a well-preserved parquet floor. The fabric on the rocker chair in the foreground also overlays the floor-length, round table cloth.

The look is Provençal in this kitchen nook where a checked table cloth jollies up a simple table. A wooden 'trolley' – with a solid top to be used as a chopping block or cutting board, and a lower shelf for storage – is pushed against the wall for convenience.

A suite among the treetops offers an elevated, private paradise. This bedroom with its own living area boasts glorious floor-to-ceiling windows to let in the sunshine. And there's always something seductive about having a fireplace in your bedroom.

Texture reigns supreme in this compact bedroom where a pile of generously sized cushions and matching silken-textured bedspread invite one to shut out the world and snooze.

LEFT: An intricately carved cherrywood archway and wall panels – imported from London – are a feature of this highly unusual dining room, where a fully mirrored wall reinforces the impression of spacious grandeur. Most remarkable of all are the half-moon and round porthole windows – with marine-inspired porcelain surrounds – which were built to recall a long-ago shipwreck, after which the house is named.

BELOW: An authentic, Cape-Dutch kitchen boasts an original fireplace adorned by copper pots and blue-and-white china. The door and the solid lintel are also original features.

This bedroom also offers a bath with a view. Natural light and neutral tones create a soothing, serene space. Beautiful wooden beams, treated cretestone walls and a floor consisting of large, unobtrusive tiles contribute to the pleasing simplicity. Texture plays an important role – from the walls and floor to the waffle-weave and knits of the bed linen and cushions. A drawer beneath the bed offers additional storage space. Candles stacked beside the bath indicate romantic nights and a simple blind offers privacy when it is desired.

The bed's the thing in this room which unashamedly calls back the past. Retro French opulence contrasts with country thatch and natural fibre carpeting. An over-the-top half-canopy almost reaches the thatched roof from which it is suspended. Imported antiques are everywhere. Set within the drape of the fully lined curtains, reading lamps suggest cosy winter evenings curled up with a good book. On the papered walls, simply framed water-colours are symmetrically placed above pleated lampshades and delicate china plates.

A dramatic chequerboard pattern is used effectively in this dining area – without it becoming overpowering. Ensuring this, only some of the restored antique chairs were upholstered in the bold black-and-white diamond fabric. The pale turquoise glass insets at the corners of the large windows add an original touch, repeating the design based on squares.

CLOCKWISE, FROM TOP LEFT:
The cool feel of a dark-brick floor is counteracted by warmth generated by an abundant use of wood in this entrance hall. At the end of the passage, sunlight beckons from the sitting room-cum-bar (shown on page 65).

The elegant, intricately made stone surround of the fireplace is complemented by the formal, oval mirror and the display of finely framed family photographs. In juxtaposition, the eye is drawn to the much simpler shapes and techniques reflected in the African curios.

The roughly hewn walls of this country pantry offer a rustic setting and provide carefully designed recesses for storing wine and household items.

The front door opens onto a splendid staircase which emphasizes the double-volume space. Granite, weathered marble tiles and a gold banister add to the feeling of grandeur. The attention is drawn upstairs by a splendid window and a small but fascinating balcony.

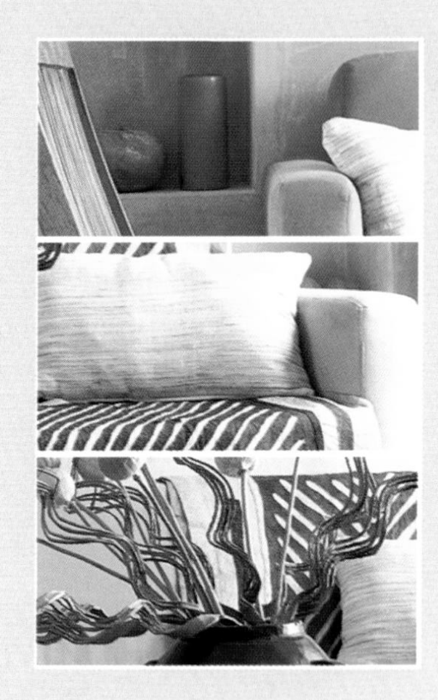

Desert hues have been used here to create a peaceful retreat. Large easy-to-clean ceramic tiles, carefully waxed cretestone walls and wooden furniture blend perfectly with the pale fabric of the couch. Hand-woven cloth is framed simply between two sheets of glass, and recessed shelves containing selected ornaments extend right to the ceiling.

In the same home as that featured on the opposite page, all-important natural light is provided by large windows, set above the eye level of passers-by outside. Kuba cloth and silk cushion covers blend with the muted tones of the colour scheme, which is even adhered to in terms of books and treasured objects displayed in the wide shelf recesses.

This is truly a rainbow room for the adventurous. Throwing caution to the wind, the owner of this kitchen has indulged in multi-coloured eccentricity. Purples, blues and a dash of pink speak loudly – even the tiled work-surface is a similar bold shade. Dragged paint techniques have been applied to the cupboards and door, and the walls have been colourwashed in pale lilac. A hard-wearing slate floor is easy to maintain. Overhead, a multi-functional suspended grid is used to display arrays of dried plants and a trusted, true blue enamel lamp.

The kitchen on the opposite page leads into a similarly vibrant dining room. The kitchen colours are reiterated with a touch of lime added in the upholstery of the mismatched wooden chairs. Sections of the legs of the chairs have been highlighted in silver. The vivid, roughly ragged walls are accentuated by shocking pink uplighters. A comparatively plain, distressed pale silver table offers light relief – and, from the ceiling, understated lamps hang at a convenient height for diners.

Rock from the surrounding area was incorporated in building this sanctuary in Mpumalanga. The compact home misleads one to believing it to be larger than it really is. The ground floor consists of a lounge-cum-dining room with a minute kitchen nook, while a bedroom incorporating a free-standing bath occupies the top floor.

The pink building in the foreground is a separate guest suite. Planters on the wall flank the V-shaped bay window, inside which a free-standing fireplace can be seen.

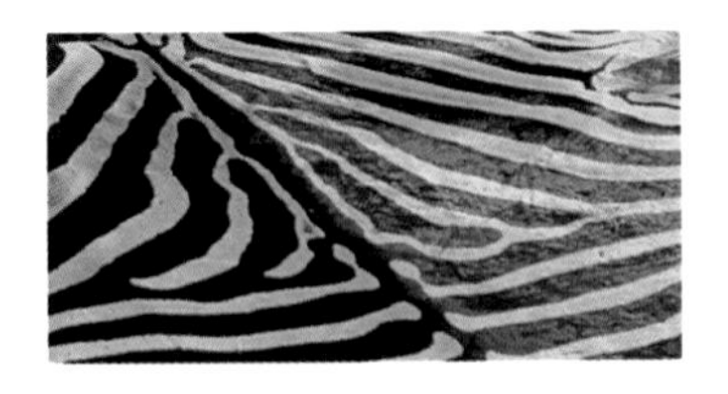

Loft living African country style sums up the design of this living-cum-sleeping area. Roughly hewn gum poles, thatch and grass are combined with hand-crafted furniture and fittings to create a uniquely natural environment. The spacious double-volume living room – in keeping with the overall style of the dwelling – is sparsely furnished, while the upstairs bed is simply adorned by a functional and decorative mosquito net. In the absence of glass, windows and some doors consist of simple hatches constructed from saplings. When the hatch in the bedroom is raised, natural light pours in past a fringe of thatch. When the hatches are closed, light and air still filter through, allowing much-needed ventilation – especially during hot, African summers – and creating patterns of light that echo nature's own design in the zebra-skin on the floor.

FAR LEFT: A corner in the reception area of this home displays some of the owner's choice collectibles. Beneath a steel staircase, a high-backed chair is dwarfed by a tall cactus. A warm-toned rug on the tiled floor creates a homely atmosphere.

LEFT, TOP: Dark oak panelling is the dominant feature of this dining room. Equally impressive woodwork is evident in the antique table and chairs and in the elegant doors with leaded glass. Only the leopard-print upholstery adds a contemporary touch to this old-world environment.

LEFT, BOTTOM: This warm lounge-cum-bar area with a strong country feel (also seen from the entrance hall on page 57, top left), combines leather, wood and cane under a sloping thatch roof. When the grass blinds are raised, dappled sunlight streams in through glass sliding doors.

It's back to basics here, where the function of the room cannot be mistaken. A bath and a shower are the total focus. Spaces between the floor-boards are designed to direct the water to a sloping floor and outlet underneath. The black, free-standing bath matches the dark floor and overlooks a wildly overgrown garden. Although roller blinds can grant privacy, steel-framed windows extending from floor to ceiling encourage bathers to enjoy the feeling of being at one with nature.

What more could one ask for: a still day, a comfortable wicker chair, a wooden deck where you can kick off your boots, and trees for Africa?

CLOCKWISE, FROM TOP LEFT: Tartan fabric in contrasting colours is used to upholster some formal armchairs, and to cover scatter cushions. A loose floral arrangement injects a burst of colour, and draws the eye to the display of lovely silver and glass collectibles.

Muted colours create a restful, formal bedroom. A quiet floral motif has been used in the curtains and duvet cover.

Rustic hues abound – even in the unusual assortment of beaded bags and trinkets on the wall. The texture of the knitted throw and cushions suits the earthy atmosphere.

A tailored look is achieved in this bedroom with its padded headboard and neat duvet.

OPPOSITE PAGE: A sense of the drama of a bygone era prevails in this lavish bedroom, where attention to detail is paramount. An extravagantly dressed antique four-poster displays an intricately crocheted bedspread and eye-catching, round, needlepoint cushions.

GLOBAL

GLOBAL

PREVIOUS SPREAD: On balmy days, the inhabitants of this house make the most of the surrounding countryside by opening doors and windows onto the extensive verandas.

ABOVE: Ample-sized armchairs, a fireplace, and an animal hide on the floor underscore the simplicity of this unpretentious living room. Rough, industrial finishes contrast with the white furniture and the romantic black-and-white Spanish shawl.

RIGHT: In this horse-lover's home, where riding boots are always at the ready, a unique work space is created by ingeniously incorporating a giant corrugated-iron drum.

This stark, uncluttered dining room looks out onto giant cacti and an imposing tree through uncurtained floor-to-ceiling doors of metal and glass. Additional natural light pours in through a pair of windows set at ceiling height on each side of the room. A row of bare light bulbs hangs high above the polished wooden table top. In contrast to the smooth, glossy wood, the table legs echo the feel of the rough pillars flanking the area and the texture of the raw, untreated floor.

OPPOSITE PAGE, LEFT: The stone surround of the fireplace is the central focus in this double-volume living room. High windows with semi-circular, spoked arches draw the eye and admit ample natural light into the room. The addition of rocking chairs creates a cosy, cottagey feel.

OPPOSITE PAGE, RIGHT: Rich, earthy tones and materials set the scene. The warm hues of wood used in the heavy front door are repeated in the wide, dark planks on the floor, which contrast with the pebbles. In terms of the overall design, arches and curves are used to contrast with straight lines.

LEFT: A leopard skin with black edging dominates the wall in a room perhaps best described as Boere-baroque. The jewel-bright colours of the cushions on the bench are a pleasing juxtaposition.

The relationship between space and light rules in this open-plan, partially double-volume, living-cum-dining area. A warm timber floor echoes the A-frame ceiling above the sleeping deck, and gives continuity to the downstairs rooms which each have their own signature in terms of furnishings – leather and wood in the living room, and wrought iron in the dining area. A pair of well-worn denim jeans pinned above the staircase tells a personal story.

LEFT, TOP: The entrance hall shown on page 74 offers a taste of what's to come. It opens into a spacious living room, unbounded by walls. Rich textures and warm tones combine to create a mellow comfort zone, where matte and gloss finishes interact and natural materials dominate.

LEFT, BOTTOM: A signature element of the design of this home is the carefully planned recessed shelving employed throughout. Wooden doors front recesses containing a television set and sound equipment, while open shelves are used to display an array of loved objects.

ABOVE: A quaint piglet marks the spot for the kitchen towels and an apron on the roughly textured wall.

RIGHT: Similar colours, designs and textures to those used in the entrance hall and living room of the home featured on the previous page are carried through to the kitchen. Recessed shelving is again a feature, as is the juxtaposition of curves and straight lines.

An elegant, sophisticated look is achieved with smooth finishes and conservative furnishings in this lounge-cum-dining room. The couch is upholstered in an attractive floral fabric which is enhanced by a vase full of beautiful garden flowers (inset).

The white paint used on the frames, shutters and surrounds of the characterful sash windows – in sharp contrast to the dark, aged stone walls – is part of what creates the charming country appeal of this home.

living at the beach

THE NOTION OF THE SEASIDE CONJURES UP different things for different people, but most South Africans probably equate it with holidays or weekend getaways. Capetonians have long boasted their claim to coastal proximity, but other provinces also offer perfect seaside living – with the added advantage of warmer water for recreational sport. For a lucky few, the beach residence is home; for some it's a second home, while for others, the option of sampling the growing number of excellent seaside guest houses is the ideal solution to lazy days on the beach without responsibility. Whether contemplating a luxury house in Plettenberg Bay or a tiny bungalow at Southbroom – there's little doubt that living beside the sea is, for most, synonymous with a great escape.

PAGE 82: From the attic room of this on-the-beach abode one feels you can see forever.

PAGE 83: Whether for breakfast or sipping sundowners, this is the perfect spot.

CLOCKWISE, FROM TOP LEFT: This basic bathroom is the epitome of elegantly 'shabby' chic. Painted wood panelling requires little upkeep, and a lamp on the sill creates magical bathtimes at night.

Despite looking like a work in progress, this bathroom meets the owners' modern, minimalist expectations. The partially bare ceiling echoes other parts of the house (as featured on pages 42, 43 and 45).

An attractive, custom-made wooden unit captures the attention and offers practical storage space in this bathroom given warmth by the presence of several timber hues.

Pale aquamarine is an ideal seaside shade – used here in the wood panelling, shutters, bath sheet and handmade soap.

PREVIOUS PAGE: This is a living room which could easily be mistaken for an art gallery. Built-in seating in the sunken lounge is a focal point in an area where everything from *objets* to furnishings and paint is kept to pale, neutral tones. The high, sloping ceiling adds further interest and airiness in a room drenched in natural light.

RIGHT: Every beach house needs a cosy room for whiling away those occasional misty, grey days. These sofas are casually covered in black and white checks and stripes, but the priority is clear with a telescope trained on the view.

CLOCKWISE, FROM TOP LEFT: The sturdy basin in this modern, mostly monochrome bathroom is simple and functional. The huge mirror not only reflects light, but gives the illusion of a much bigger space.

Serene simplicity – a white wicker chair faces the view on this covered deck. A neutral blind keeps out the sun but not the scenery, and pale aquamarine shutters add a touch of class.

The owners have used the blue-and-white theme to good effect in this double-volume area. Kids have a ball in these beds, with plenty of room above each bunk. Intriguing triangular windows contribute to the light and spacious feel.

A practical, sturdy balustrade on this deck obstructs neither the awesome view, nor the cool breeze off the sea.

One can imagine extended families congregating in favourite spots in this spacious lounge. A pair of striped armchairs near a window provides comfort and light for readers, floral upholstery creates a cosy corner for conversationalists, and the couch calls out to those who are content to do nothing but watch the fire or play a game of chess on the table in front of them.

RIGHT: There's no reason why a passion for hunting cannot be reflected in a beach house, as illustrated here in the use of animal hides and heads. Windows aplenty admit light and scatter cushions inject stripes of colour. A selection of well-worn furniture lends home-from-home appeal.

OPPOSITE PAGE: Making no concessions for the camera, this is a room with a relaxed, holiday feel. Brick walls are given a rough coat of white paint, bed linen is mismatched, and frequently used sun hats in a wicker basket are stored under an aged wooden table. Even the pictures on the wall have been hung without much concern for symmetry or straight lines.

Suitably hinged doors are able to open wide, and huge windows in the simplest of wooden frames bring the uninterrupted scenery into this corner, where lunch is set for two. In seeming acknowledgment of nature's simple perfection, furniture is uncomplicated and unadorned.

CLOCKWISE, FROM TOP LEFT:
A frequently used hand-painted message invites family and friends to follow.

The elements have added character to the woodwork of this covered deck, which presents a choice spot for enjoying the picture-postcard setting and listening to the sound of the sea.

Welcome to a private bit of heaven. An open gate shows you where to go.

This is but one charming aspect of a beach cottage where dainty flowers punctuate the pretty white-painted wooden structures.

RIGHT: Basic roller blinds keep out the sun behind a comfy sofa protected by dark brown patterned throws. A cane lampshade on a dark base matches the clay pots and an ornate but empty frame does not look out of place.

OPPOSITE PAGE: The beach beckons late risers in the same house as that shown on previous pages. The finishes and details are repeated here – from the wooden window-frames, to the wood-panelled walls and roller blinds. Blue and white echo the colours and feel of the sea and the sand.

It's a case of comfort without clutter in this living room, where dark ceiling beams contrast with painted wood panelling. The simplicity is sustained throughout the house, as can be seen on the previous pages, on page 92 and – from an outdoor perspective – on page 82.

Windows set in simple, varnished, wooden frames are lightly screened with blinds. Beige throws protect removable slip-covers on the sofas, which seem to invite an afternoon snooze.

ABOVE: A beautiful corner unit of blonde wood draws the attention. Frequently used holiday items are haphazardly hung on convenient hooks, the lower row of which is cleverly placed at 'child height'. Pale aquamarine accents are visible in the fabric on the chair, in the towel, the skirting board, the shutter and in the bundle of wooden fish hanging below the arched mirror.

RIGHT: Kitchen utensils are suspended from a chrome rod for easy access, and an old wooden table displays other finds. Buckets and a tin bath stored underneath are at the ready for cleaning freshly caught fish and washing shells.

This is the same highly functional kitchen as that seen from a different angle on the opposite page. Economical, yet effective artistic touches are visible in the washed cupboards, the rectangular painting above the window, and the single agapanthus.

SUGAR
SAGO
RAISINS

OPPOSITE PAGE: A perfect seaside colour choice, soft aquamarine comes into its own in these custom-built kitchen units. The same shade is incorporated throughout the house and is also visible on page 84 in the bathroom and in the shutters on page 87. Delicate, dried starfish – used as a decorative detail on the lampshade – reinforce the coastal identity of the home.

FAR LEFT: A wooden double-storey getaway imposes minimally on the natural habitat.

LEFT, TOP: The blue trim along the fascia boards of this house – first seen on page 82 – gives it a distinctive finish and links the roof treatment to the blue door and window-frames. The feel is cool and clean, in keeping with the surroundings.

LEFT, BOTTOM: A well-used, comfortable armchair extends an invitation to visitors to warm themselves in the sun.

LEFT: Under the milkwood . . . what is revealed is a much-coveted shaded corner on Third Beach, Clifton, with built-in seating for lunch and a pair of comfortable loungers for the daily siesta thereafter.

OPPOSITE PAGE: Only the roof was left intact during the renovation of this house on Third Beach, Clifton (also featured on this page). Despite the population density in this sought-after area, the architect created a magnificent, private haven right on the beach. The balustrade style used for the balcony off the main bedroom is repeated on top of a wall constructed from rocks excavated from the original site. Granite boulders provide additional boundary 'walls' and lush foliage makes up for the absence of a more 'conventional' garden. A retractable ladder (next to the boulder) provides a clever shortcut down to the beach.

Here is another view of the lounge featured on page 85. From the other side of the room one sees beyond the sunken seating area. The exposed rafters were lightly sanded to achieve an integrated look overall.

TOP LEFT AND BOTTOM RIGHT: Carefully planned angles and utter simplicity are in keeping with the style of the home at Third Beach, Clifton (also seen on pages 85, and 102 to 105). In a corner of the bathroom, the basin – a generously sized, sand-blasted glass bowl – rests elegantly atop a built-in cupboard. Small, white tiles are used extensively – in creating an unusual, specially constructed bath, on the floor and up the walls to the ceiling. Built-in wooden shelves store towels, and others display exquisite ceramics.

TOP RIGHT AND BOTTOM LEFT: A clean, no-nonsense white bathroom with touches of blue suits the house also featured on page 87 (bottom right). Painted wood panelling is continued here, and large, easy-to-clean tiles cover the floor. The unusual soapdish was a lucky find.

Self-confessed workaholics, the owners of this Clifton beach house incorporated desk space into their bedroom. Once again, they opted for built-in units, which also display treasured ceramics. Easily washable slip-covers transform the chairs and integrate them into the decor. The shining floor has an easy-care wood veneer finish. Throughout the house, the sloping ceilings and recessed downlighters are important design features.

The work space on the previous page is seen here from the bedroom area, from which it can be separated completely by closing the sliding door. Generous curtains fall softly to the floor, which is carpeted in natural fibre matting. A practical bolster props up the pillows and extendable bedside lights adapt to personal needs.

A hard-wearing chequerplate aluminium floor sets the tone in this kitchen which is one of two in the Clifton beach house. The owners chose stainless steel in combination with white-washed, ash cabinets. Cupboard doors in the dining area and the sliding door – which shuts off the clutter after mealtimes – are made of sand-blasted glass.

One way to sort out the kids and their friends when you are on holiday is to throw them all together in this double-decker bedroom. The runged ladders at the sides – fronting the shelf spaces – lead to the sleeping-room-only upper deck. For those so inclined, individually controlled lights allow for a late-night read without disturbing roommates. And for good measure, all the toys and other kids' paraphernalia can be stowed away in drawers beneath the expanse of the giant bed.

An extremely high ceiling with exposed beams makes a strong statement in this room where the owner acknowledges an Indonesian influence. The coffee table is in fact an antique weaving table from Bali. The mirror has been set in a carved frame from Thailand, while the lime-washed lattice cupboards on either side of the fireplace were custom-made.

CLOCKWISE, FROM TOP LEFT: Eastern influences continue in the bathroom of the same house featured opposite. The unusual bath, placed on a plinth, was moulded according to the owner's specifications.

In the absence of cut flowers, shells and starfish have been used to complement driftwood in a delicate arrangement.

A buffet drawer unit imported from Bali has pride of place at the opposite end of the lounge featured on the opposite page. The rough look of the wall was achieved by plastering it with cement mixed with lime, and leaving it unpainted.

This bed was made for dreaming . . . in complete luxury. Beneath the exposed thatch roof, the feel is romantic. Pretty bed linen and soft, white drapes elegantly adorn the large four-poster.

RIGHT: If the wind keeps you off the beach, this is a perfect, private corner for intimate conversations or relaxing with a favourite magazine. The blue touches used throughout the house (seen on pages 87, 106 and 115) are repeated in the cushions on the chunky, grey chairs. The unusual, triangular windows – a feature of this house – are visible once again.

OPPOSITE PAGE: The lounge of the same dwelling pictured on this page offers homely comfort and richer colours. The same vibrant shade of blue seen in other areas of the house reappears here in printed fabric and stripes. The shocking pink of the easy chair and occasional scatter cushions adds fun and surprise. And on a cool evening, the wood at the ready in the fireplace only needs a match to light a fire for toasting marshmallows!

living outdoors

FOR MANY PEOPLE, THE IDEA OF SPENDING TIME OUTDOORS means leaving their home environment. In the context of this book, however, outdoor living will be explored, not with regard to outings and holiday trips, but in terms of how everyday house and garden design can provide for outdoor enjoyment. South Africans are particularly fortunate, because, in most parts of the country, for the greater part of the year, we are treated to glorious weather. With clever planning, many of us need not leave home to find a spot for soaking up the sun, looking at the sunset, marvelling at the colours of a distant mountain, or enjoying the shade of a tree. From tiny nooks, crannies and balconies to lavish outdoor entertainment areas such as verandas, decks, patios, or pool surrounds – here are ideas aplenty.

PAGE 116: Large, leafy trees and ivy-covered walls add to the charm of this alfresco dining area. A striped, canvas awning and additional curtains ensure shelter. Even the steps are used as a design feature, bordered by potted plants on either side.This theme is carried through to the pool, where pots with beautiful plants adorn the corners.

CLOCKWISE, FROM TOP LEFT: Quintessentially English in style, this unstructured meadow garden has standard Iceberg roses lending height to the contrasting green foliage and the yellow, purple and white flowers beside the slate-roofed pool house.

Even a tiny, decorative cast-iron balcony can afford a flat-dweller a magnificent view.

Purple pansies catch the eye in lush greenery. The border of old Cape pavers gives a neat outline to the stone pathway.

Wonderful willows form massive natural umbrellas in a vast Vaal River garden.

The owners of this home wanted the outdoors to be very much part of their lives as witnessed here, where only a sliding door separates the sitting room from an autumnal scene. With the door open, a deck of old railway sleepers allows direct access to the koi pond, and the countless trees and shrubs become part of the decor.

The feel is almost that of a palazzo in Venice where a black-and-white pole looks set to moor the gondola. Bold use of colour creates a bright, cheerful atmosphere, softened by the subtle introduction of greens and blues. The add-on conservatory (at the right of the photograph) introduces a totally different style and texture to the building. The furniture is natural cane.

ABOVE: Wrought-iron bar stools with a tinge of verdigris – and a delicate grape motif – complement the outdoor bar area of the house featured on the opposite page. On the counter, real fruit is displayed alongside the ornamental kind. A retractable awning provides optional shade-cover.

RIGHT: Romeo and Juliet's romantic liaison would not be out of place in this theatrical setting. A colonnaded balcony is in keeping with the Italian style of the architecture. Majestic arches and pillars seem almost to rise from the still water of the pool, in which they are reflected. In the middle of the patio – beneath the table – tiles have been laid to create a discreet circular design.

PREVIOUS SPREAD: A breath-taking view of Hout Bay harbour and Chapman's Peak is one of the perks of this magnificent property. To impinge as little as possible on the natural environment, original pine trees have been retained – as has the natural rock which becomes a feature of the pool. Loungers with cushions covered in African cloth invite sun-worshippers to take it all in.

RIGHT: An appealing porch setting makes an ideal outdoor dining area – equally suited to breakfast, lunch or supper. Striped, tie-on cushions adorn the chairs, which, like the table, are made of high-quality, durable wood. An established garden in the background is a bonus while, under cover, creepers are still in training. In the interim, variegated foliage and mostly white impatiens provide the floral decor.

A cup of coffee and a croissant, a crossword puzzle and a pair of binoculars for bird-watching seem like a good way to start the day. Comfortable-looking, dark green cushions on sturdy iron chairs enhance the verdant scenery in this shady corner, where a large conifer reaches upward among the potted Iceberg roses.

OPPOSITE PAGE: The familiar gabled, Cape Dutch style of architecture is encountered at this expansive dwelling in Stellenbosch. The two-tone brick surround of the pool is softened by ferns in this area ideal for entertaining guests.

LEFT: A life-sized bronze sculpture of a dancer appears to pirouette on a platform at the top end of this pool. A tropical backdrop – planted with an eye for symmetry – is provided by banana and palm trees, which also offer some privacy and shelter.

FOLLOWING SPREAD: This family home, designed by its owner and built three years ago, was inspired by plantation houses seen on Mauritius. All the outside doors open onto the manicured lawn. The extensive veranda was constructed to accommodate an ancient, protected oak tree, and conservatories were erected on two sides of the house. The main bedroom occupies the entire second floor and looks out onto an unpopulated green belt.

CLOCKWISE, FROM TOP LEFT:
Cane chairs with comfortable, bulky cushions entice one to tea – elegantly served in the family silver. Lovely cut flowers are casually arranged.

A covered stoep is an ideal look-out point for keeping an eye on the kids at play on the grass. A grape vine entwines itself round a pergola and a low hedge of scented lavender snuggles against the stoep.

Colour is the main ingredient in this outdoor setting where sunflowers liven up an already jolly table. The blue-and-white checked table mats, fruit-shaped napkin rings and the cobalt blue glasses and vase are an inspiring combination.

A warm and sheltered spot on the veranda supplies sun-bleached wooden loungers for long, lazy afternoons.

A strong oriental influence is discernible in this leafy, green garden which substitutes a combination of light and dark shades of gravel for a lawn. Vertical interest is supplied by the architecture and also by the forest of old and young trees. The slate surround – while adding definition to the shape of the house – does nothing to interrupt the indoor–outdoor flow.

RIGHT: There's an air of formality about the wooden table and chairs next to the trelliswork in this covered poolside dining area. The long, dark pool – ideal for serious swimmers – is given a plain, functional brick surround. Moss-dappled pots are the only decorative elements apart from the natural garden foliage.

OPPOSITE PAGE: In creating this bush camp in Mpumalanga, architects opted for indigenous materials and unusual design. In the lapa, a fence made of extraordinarily shaped, dry bush-willow 'poles' creates an almost surreal atmosphere. Wooden chairs, made locally, are arranged on the sand around the central, stone-mosaic braai. Constant discoveries of a fascinating array of sculpted shapes are a never-ending source of delight, and a winding pathway leads up the rocky slope to a sheltered look-out point.

CLOCKWISE, FROM TOP LEFT:
Nothing distracts from this visual feast of clear blue water and sky. In place of a solid slab pool surround, a combination of square pavers and large white pebbles create interest.

Sun exposure is controlled by a pulley at the Clifton home featured on previous pages. The distressed floor, pots and pebbles echo the shades and textures of the beach setting.

From the porch of this home at Misty Cliffs, near Scarborough in the Cape, one can hear the sound of the sea and the gulls, and watch the breakers through painted wooden arches.

Another view of the same Clifton home (top right) reveals the natural rock excavated from the site – used here to build steps, in combination with washed timber planks. Pots filled with young lavender bushes soften the lines of the balustrade.

TOP LEFT AND RIGHT, AND BOTTOM LEFT: Architectural surprises and concern for texture and design give this city house its originality. Apart from the plants, colour has been limited to grey, white and black. While minimalist in approach, attention to detail is evident everywhere. The solidity of the wall behind the bamboo plants is 'broken' by a space. An angular twist contributes to an aesthetically pleasing balcony. The clean, horizontal lines of the staircase make for an impressive front entrance, where the steel door is also a special feature.

BOTTOM RIGHT: Minimal maintenance is a by-product of the design of this garden landscape, where the dark silhouette of a sculpted African figurine contrasts with and overlooks an abundance of white and grey pebbles. An elevated earthenware pot recalls the decor inside the house (seen on pages 85, 104, 107 and 108). The dots of colour provided by the violets are a surprising, welcome element in this garden of stones.

LEFT: Uplighters and a low wall make the most of the pretty street façade of this Cape Victorian residence, which typifies the Huguenot influence in the Cape winelands, and is exactly as it was over a hundred years ago. Sash windows and thatch roofs were the order of the day, and remain an architectural preference for many new houses in the area. Dainty flowers and Iceberg roses add a touch of white to the otherwise green garden, which includes shapely conifers in wooden half-barrels.

FOLLOWING PAGE: Symmetry rules in this sunny, sheltered courtyard where identical shuttered windows upstairs and downstairs look onto neat patches of grass bordered by brick surrounds and gravel. Two large, identical wall-lanterns flank the entrance, as do two identically shaped trees in pots. Only the doors, one above the other, differ in design. The colours used on the walls and woodwork – predominantly creamy peach and pale grey – seem to have become almost faded by the power of the strong sunlight.

CLOCKWISE, FROM TOP LEFT: The house featured on the opposite page offers a host of sheltered hideaways. Candles on the slim table against the wall indicate the possibility of intimate tête-à-têtes on warm evenings. A bowl of lemons on the stone-topped wrought-iron table hints at pre-dinner drinks and cocktails.

Beyond the large, glass-paned doors, an antique wooden chair encourages a private moment of meditation on this covered veranda.

A solid wood and rattan chair invites one to lie back and enjoy the vineyards and scenic wonderland visible beyond the bed of indigenous agapanthus.

Elsewhere along the same tin-roofed veranda, the eye is presented with a captivating mountain view. Cane and wooden chairs await the sociable, while in the distance a pair of loungers provides an opportunity for spending time away from the crowd.

CLOCKWISE, FROM TOP LEFT: Sturdy iron garden furniture on a base of old railway sleepers is pleasing and unpretentious.

Taking on the challenge of a house built on a steep slope and in poor soil conditions, the owners of this home compensated by creating a steep rock garden packed with appropriate plants. A grey stone birdbath with an aged look invites bird life.

The relaxed charm of this all-white entrance is enhanced by the shrubs, greenery and flowers which spill over the wall and gate. The weathered-looking stairs add character.

This serene, secluded spot in a sprawling Magaliesberg garden inspires contemplation or romance. An archway offers intrigue behind a willow tree which dips into the lily pond.

A magenta bougainvillaea forms a natural awning outside this antique-filled sitting room. In the background, a fountain soothes the senses and an urn sprouts greenery atop a plinth in the recessed wall. Floral linen is an appropriate choice for covering cushions used on outdoor furniture.

The owners of this Vaal River residence have thrown concerns about privacy and security to the wind in their appreciation and celebration of an incomparable setting where willows weep at water's edge, a still pool mirrors the sky, and loungers are at the ready both on the lawn and on the covered viewing terrace.

credits

(t=top b=bottom l=left r=right)
(Arch=Architect Prod=Production
Dec=Decor St=Styling)

cover, front	Arch: Richard Tremeer
cover, back, l	Archs: Richard Tremeer & John Jacobson Prod: Shelley Street
cover, back, r	Arch: Sylvio Rech
p.1	Arch: Greg Wright Styling: Sonja Nel
pp. 2/3	Arch: Stefan Antoni
p. 4	Arch: John Jacobson/Metropolis
p. 6	Arch: Greg Wright
p. 8	Prod: Tina-Marié Malherbe Dec: Laing McLaren
p. 10 t & r	Prod: Tina-Marié Malherbe
p. 11 main	Arch: Richard Tremeer
p. 11 inset	Arch & Dec: Stefan Antoni
p. 12	Prod: Shelley Street
p. 13	Archs: Richard Tremeer & John Jacobson Prod: Shelley Street
p. 14 tl	Arch: Richard Tremeer St: Shelley Street
p. 14 tr	Prod: Tina-Marié Malherbe Dec: Shelley Street
p. 14 br	Arch & Dec: Stefan Antoni
p. 14 bl	Prod: Tina-Marié Malherbe
p. 15	Arch: Richard Tremeer
pp. 16/17	Dec: Rocco Bosman St: Sonja Nel
p. 18	Arch: Stefan Antoni
p. 19	Prod: Tina-Marié Malherbe Dec: Laing McLaren
p. 20	St: Shelley Street
p. 21 tl, bl & br	Prod: Shelley Street
p. 21 tr	St: Shelley Street
p. 22	Arch: Stefan Antoni
p. 23	Prod: Tina-Marié Malherbe Dec: Shelley Street
p. 24	Arch: Stéphan Weyers Architects
p. 25 l	Arch: Richard Tremeer St: Shelley Street
p. 25 tr	Arch & Dec: Bert Pepler St: Sonja Nel
p. 25 br	Dec: Rocco Bosman St: Sonja Nel
p. 26	Arch & Dec: Anya Miszewski
p. 27	Arch & Dec: Anya Miszewski
pp. 28/29	Arch & Dec: Anya Miszewski
p. 30	Arch: Richard Tremeer St: Shelley Street
p. 31	Archs: Richard Tremeer & John Jacobson St: Shelley Street
pp. 32/33	Archs: Stefan Antoni Prod: Elaine Levitte
p. 34	Arch: Alfio Torrisi
p. 35	Arch: Leon Savin Prod: Shelley Street
p. 36 inset	Dec: Rocco Bosman
p. 36 main	Arch & Dec: Bert Pepler St: Sonja Nel
p. 37 all	Arch: Bert Pepler St: Sonja Nel
p. 38	Dec: Stephen Rich
p. 39	Dec: Stephen Rich
p. 40	Prod: Shelley Street
p. 41	Dec: Guillermo Lapidus
p. 42	Arch: Greg Wright
p. 43 both	Arch: Greg Wright
p. 44	Arch: Stéphan Weyers Architects
p. 45 l	Arch: Greg Wright
p. 45 r, t & b	Arch: Stéphan Weyers Architects
p. 46	Dec: Gill Gage
p. 48	Arch: Luis Ferreira Da Silva
p. 49	Arch: Luis Ferreira Da Silva
p. 50	Arch: Luis Ferreira Da Silva
p. 51	Dec: Uschi Stuart
p. 52 tl	Prod: Tina-Marié Malherbe Dec: Veronique Gussman
p. 52 tr	Dec: Tracy Rehr
p. 52 br	Dec: Dorothy Van't Riet
p. 52 bl	Arch: Stéphan Weyers Architects Dec: Elize Boezaard
p. 53 inset	Dec: Gill Gage
p. 54	Prod: Tina-Marié Malherbe Dec: Uschi Stuart
p. 55	Dec: Guillaume Decorators
p. 56	Arch: Luis Ferreira Da Silva
p. 57 tl	Dec: Uschi Stuart
p. 57 tr	Dec: Tracy Rehr
p. 57 br	Arch & Dec: Sylvio Rech
p. 57 bl	Arch: Luis Ferreira Da Silva
p. 58	Dec: Uschi Stuart
p. 59	Dec: Uschi Stuart
p. 60	St: Shelley Street
p. 61	St: Shelley Street
pp. 62/63	Arch: Luis Ferreira Da Silva
p. 64	Arch: Sylvio Rech
p. 65 br	Dec: Uschi Stuart
p. 66	Archs: Richard Tremeer & John Jacobson St: Sonja Nel
p. 67	Archs: Richard Tremeer & John Jacobson St: Sonja Nel
p. 68 tl	Dec: Tracy Rehr
p. 68 tr	Dec: Gill Gage
p. 68 br	Dec: Uschi Stuart
p. 68 bl	Dec: Gill Gage
p. 69	Dec: Guillaume Decorators
p. 72 main	St: Sonja Nel
p. 72 inset	St: Sonja Nel
p. 73	St: Sonja Nel
p. 74 l	St: Sonja Nel
p. 74 r	Arch: Stéphan Weyers Architects Dec: Elize Boezaard
p. 75	St: Sonja Nel
p. 76	Arch: Stéphan Weyers Architects
p. 77 t	Arch: Stéphan Weyers Architects Dec: Elize Boezaard
p. 77 b	Arch: Stéphan Weyers Architects Dec: Elize Boezaard
p. 78	Arch: Stéphan Weyers Architects Dec: Elize Boezaard
p. 79	Dec: Gill Gage
p. 83	Arch: Stefan Antoni
p. 84 tl	St: Sonja Nel
p. 84 tr	Arch: Greg Wright St: Sonja Nel
p. 84 br	St: Sonja Nel
p. 85	Arch: John Jacobson/Metropolis
p. 86	St: Sonja Nel
p. 87 tl	Arch & Dec: Anya Miszewski
p. 87 br	Sunset Beach Guest House, Noordhoek
p. 87 bl	Arch: Bert Pepler St: Sonja Nel
p. 90	St: Sonja Nel
p. 91	St: Sonja Nel
p. 92	St: Sonja Nel
p. 93 tr	St: Sonja Nel
p. 94	St: Sonja Nel
p. 95	St: Sonja Nel
pp. 96/97	St: Sonja Nel
p. 98 main	St: Sonja Nel
p. 99	St: Sonja Nel
p. 101 br	St: Sonja Nel
p. 102	Arch: John Jacobson/Metropolis
p. 103	Arch: John Jacobson/Metropolis
pp. 104/105	Arch: John Jacobson/Metropolis
p. 106 tl	Arch: John Jacobson/Metropolis
p. 106 tr	Sunset Beach Guest House, Noordhoek
p. 106 br	Arch: John Jacobson/Metropolis
p. 106 bl	Sunset Beach Guest House, Noordhoek
p. 107	Arch: John Jacobson/Metropolis
pp. 108/109	Arch: John Jacobson/Metropolis
p. 110	Arch: John Jacobson/Metropolis
p. 111	Arch: John Jacobson/Metropolis
p. 112	Dec: Faline Edwards, Colours Decorators
p. 113 tl	Dec: Faline Edwards, Colours Decorators
p. 113 tr	Sunset Beach Guest House, Noordhoek
p. 113 br	Dec: Faline Edwards, Colours Decorators
p. 113 bl	Sunset Beach Guest House, Noordhoek
p. 114	Sunset Beach Guest House, Noordhoek
p. 115	Sunset Beach Guest House, Noordhoek
p. 116	Dec: Jay Smith
p. 118 tr	Prod: Tina-Marié Malherbe Dec: Veronique Gussman
p. 118 br	Arch: Anya Miszewski
p. 118 bl	Dec: Gill Gage
p. 119	Dec: Dorothy Van't Riet
p. 120	Arch: Luis Ferreira Da Silva
p. 121 l	Arch: Luis Ferreira Da Silva
p. 124	Dec: Gill Gage
p. 125	Dec: Karen Lotter
p. 126	Van der Stel Manor, Guest House, Stellenbosch
p. 127	Dec: Brian Leib
p. 130 tl	Dec: Gill Gage
p. 130 tr	St: Sonja Nel
p. 130 br	Dec: Tracy Rehr
p. 130 bl	Dec: Gill Gage
p. 131	Arch: Anya Miszewski
p. 133	Arch: Sylvio Rech
p. 134 tl	Dec: Faline Edwards, Colours Decorators
p. 134 tr	Arch: John Jacobson/Metropolis
p. 134 bl	Arch: John Jacobson/Metropolis
p. 135 tl	Arch: Greg Wright
p. 135 tr	Arch: Greg Wright
p. 135 br	Arch: John Jacobson/Metropolis
p. 135 bl	Arch: Greg Wright
p. 138	Arch: Michael Dall
p. 139 all	Arch: Michael Dall
p. 140 tl	Arch: Stéphan Weyers Architects Dec: Elize Boezaard
p. 140 tr	Arch: Michael Dall
p. 140 br	Arch: Bert Pepler
p. 140 bl	Mount Grace Hotel
p. 141	Dec: Peter Sullivan